KAREEM ABDUL-JABBAR

by
William R. Sanford
&
Carl R. Green

CRESTWOOD HOUSE
New York

Maxwell Macmillan Canada
Toronto

Maxwell Macmillan International
New York Oxford Singapore Sydney

Library of Congress Cataloging-in-Publication Data
Sanford, William R. (William Reynolds), 1927–
   Kareem Abdul-Jabbar / by William R. Sanford and Carl R. Green. — 1st ed.
     p. cm. — (Sports immortals)
   Includes bibliographical references and index.
   Summary: A biography of one of basketball's greatest stars. Includes a trivia quiz.
   ISBN 0-89686-737-4
   1. Abdul-Jabbar, Kareem, 1947– —Juvenile literature. 2. Basketball players—United States—Biography—Juvenile
literature. [1. Abdul-Jabbar, Kareem, 1947– 2. Basketball players. 3. Afro-Americans—Biography.] I. Green, Carl R.
 II. Title. III. Series.
GV884.A24S26   1993
796.323'092—dc20
[B]   92-3592

Photo Credits
All photos courtesy of The Bettmann Archive

Macmillan Publishing Company
866 Third Avenue
New York, NY 10022

Maxwell Macmillan Canada, Inc.
1200 Eglinton Avenue East
Suite 200
Don Mills, Ontario M3C 3N1

CRESTWOOD HOUSE

Macmillan Publishing Company is part of the Maxwell Communication Group of Companies.

Produced by Flying Fish Studio

Printed in the United States of America

First edition

10 9 8 7 6 5 4 3 2 1

CONTENTS

A Lesson in Basketball Manners 5

Growing Up Tall in New York City 7

Rewriting the High School Record Book 10

The Best Team on Campus 13

The UCLA Glory Days 16

Breaking In with the Pros 20

An Unhappy MVP 24

Starting Over in Los Angeles 29

Kareem Teams with Magic 33

The Final Year 37

Kareem Abdul-Jabbar, Basketball Immortal 41

Glossary 43

More Good Reading About Kareem 45

Kareem Abdul-Jabbar Trivia Quiz 46

Index 48

Few basketball players have been able to match the the skill of Lew Alcindor (better known today as Kareem Abdul-Jabbar).

A LESSON IN BASKETBALL MANNERS

Over 50,000 fans turned out to see the biggest college basketball game of 1967. Unbeaten UCLA was matched against unbeaten Houston in the Astrodome. UCLA was led by 7-foot Lew Alcindor (better known today as Kareem Abdul-Jabbar). Houston wasn't afraid of the big, bad Bruins. The Cougars had won 17 games in a row behind Elvin (Big E) Hayes.

Lew came into the big game with a double handicap. One had been created by the rules committee. An off-season decision had outlawed one of his best weapons, the **dunk shot**. Sportswriters claimed that the change had been made to take away some of Lew's height advantage. The second problem was that his left eye had been scratched eight days earlier. Could Lew keep up with the Big E after spending almost a week in the hospital?

Houston jumped out on top as Hayes hit for 29 points in the first half. UCLA's guards led a second-half rally that tied the game at 69-all. But this was Houston's night. Hayes won the game with two last-minute free throws, 71-69. Lew, who was clearly off his game, had been held to only 15 points. Afterward, Lew and his teammates began thinking about revenge.

When Kareem was a 7-foot-tall high school sophomore, Coach Jack Donohue treated him the same as he did every sophomore who played varsity basketball at Power Memorial. What chore did the coach assign to Kareem?

* Answers to all Trivia Quiz questions can be found on pages 46–47.

UCLA did not have to wait very long. Both teams won the rest of their games, setting up a rematch in the **NCAA** tournament. The winner would go on to play for the national championship. When the teams met at the Sports Arena in Los Angeles, Hayes had his mouth going as usual. "Man, we're gonna beat you," he whispered to Lew. "We're gonna beat you bad."

Lew ignored the Big E's taunts. UCLA came out running and quickly turned the Great Rematch into the Great Mismatch. When the Bruin press wasn't stealing the ball, the tight defense kept Hayes under control. In all, the Big E scored only 10 points that night, 5 in each half. For his part, Lew took control of the backboards and chipped in with his share of the scoring.

The crowd came to its feet when Lew stole the ball and dribbled to the basket. The no-dunk rule kept him from slamming the ball home as he wanted to do. But Lew was really pumped up. His elbows were *above* the rim when he soared in for his lay-up. Houston never recovered. When the buzzer sounded to end the game, UCLA was leading by 32 points, 101-69.

A night later UCLA won its second straight NCAA title by defeating North Carolina, 78-55. But the win over Houston was still on Lew's mind. "They were annoying and insulting," he said. "We wanted to teach those people some manners."

High school players tried nearly every trick in the book when they were assigned to guard Kareem during his years at Power Memorial. What did one Boys High of Brooklyn player do in a desperate attempt to stop the big center?

GROWING UP TALL IN NEW YORK CITY

The boy who grew up to be Kareem Abdul-Jabbar was born in New York City on April 16, 1947. He was big even then, weighing in at almost 13 pounds and measuring 22-1/2 inches. Al and Cora Alcindor named their only child Ferdinand Lewis Alcindor, Jr. Big Al was a fine musician who earned his living as a Transit Authority policeman. As Lew grew up, Cora made sure he paid attention to his schoolwork. Education came first in the Alcindor household.

The Alcindors moved to the Dyckman Housing Project in Manhattan when Lew was three. Lew's room looked out over Fort Tryon Park. Most of the families in Dyckman were white. When Lew started school at St. Jude's, he was one of the few blacks there. Lew says he was not aware of his race until he saw himself in a third-grade class picture. But he soon learned that blacks can be the targets of abuse. It hurt when his best friend screamed racial insults at him during a quarrel.

Lew liked sports, but he liked schoolwork too. His home was filled with books and he became an avid reader. Teachers quickly sensed that he was bright and eager to learn. The nuns at St. Jude's often asked him to read aloud to the class. That honor earned him the playground title of Teacher's Pet. Even so, other boys thought twice before they picked on Lew. By his ninth birthday he was 5 feet 4 inches tall.

Cora and Big Al sent Lew to a **boarding school** in Philadelphia when he started fourth grade. Both were working and believed he needed more care than they could give him. Lew felt out of place at Holy Providence. The tough street kids in his class teased him because he liked books and spoke good English. It was on the playground that Lew won respect. His height made him a standout in the daily basketball games. Awkward and shy at first, he soon learned to mix it up with the street kids.

When the year ended Lew was happy to return to New York. The coaches at St. Jude's were happy too. Coach Farrell Hopkins helped him overcome his awkwardness with a heavy workout program. Lew put in long hours on the court and in the weight room. When he was a seventh grader the team was given new uniforms. That was the day Lew put on number 33 for the first time. When he retired many years later, he was still wearing the same number 33.

After a summer of practice, Lew mastered the dunk shot. The fans went wild when he dunked for the first time as an eighth grader. With 6-foot-8-inch Lew leading the way, St. Jude's reached the finals of the city championships. Even though the team lost in overtime, St. Jude's students and teachers were overjoyed. The second-place trophy was given a place of honor in the school's display case.

High schools had been recruiting Lew ever since he was a seventh grader. With the help of his parents, Lew chose Power Memorial Academy. Two of his friends went to Power Memorial, and the school was strong on academics. The decision made, Lew found time to relax that summer. When he wasn't playing basketball, he hung out at Roy's Coffee Shop. The jukebox at Roy's played the kind of jazz he enjoyed.

Young Lew Alcindor shown in a Power Memorial Academy photograph

High school basketball star Lew Alcindor blocks a shot for Power.

REWRITING THE HIGH SCHOOL RECORD BOOK

Lew rode the subway to Power Memorial each day. The ride gave him time to think. Like most teenagers, he worried about being different. At the mostly white school, his height and race set him apart. At times he thought of himself as a "minority of one." Even so, Lew welcomed the strict rules and the emphasis on learning. He made the honor roll during his first semester at Power Memorial.

When basketball practice started, Lew expected to play for the junior varsity. He was amazed when Coach Jack Donohue moved him up to the varsity. In his first game, Lew was outplayed by older, stronger players. Afterward he sat in the locker room and cried. The second game was not much better. Trying too hard, Lew got into foul trouble. Coach Donohue told him, "I hope you're learning what it's all about to really want to win."

Slowly, Lew pulled his game together. By season's end he was scoring in double figures. As he improved, so did the team's record. But whenever Lew made a mistake, Donohue was there to correct him. "What are you, a farmer?" the coach would yell when Lew dropped a **rebound**. Anxious to please, Lew learned to scrap for every ball at both ends of the court. He also learned about team play. Donohue taught a disciplined style that featured passing and defense.

With a 20-win season behind him, Lew spent the summer at Donohue's basketball camp. The camp was held on a farm in upstate New York. The boys played their games on a dirt court. When they weren't practicing, they helped build cabins and swam in the Hudson River. By then Lew had grown to 6 feet 10 inches.

Power Memorial opened its 1962 season in Madison Square Garden against the city champs. Lew's natural athletic ability was catching up with his rapid growth. Coach Donohue's Panthers won the game and went on to an unbeaten season. Newspapers began to write about Lew's exploits on the court. Donohue did his best to keep reporters away from his sophomore star. He didn't want Lew to forget he was part of a team.

The Panthers' winning streak extended into Lew's junior year. The skyscraping center now topped 7 feet and weighed 220 pounds. He wore a size 16D shoe. On the court, Lew averaged

26 points a game and 18 rebounds. Off the court, his mailbox was stuffed with letters from college coaches. With Lew at center, any team would have a shot at winning a national championship.

Lew loved basketball but he did not let the game rule his life. In September 1963, four little black girls were killed in a church bombing in Alabama. Lew was enraged. He felt that the country wasn't doing enough to fight racial injustice. During an Easter trip to North Carolina, he had seen prejudice firsthand. In the South, signs that barred blacks from using white drinking fountains and rest rooms were still common.

Lew leaps into the air to make a basket for the Panthers.

In Lew's senior year, Power Memorial's win streak reached 71 before the Panthers lost a game. That was the team's only defeat during Lew's last three years. In his final game, the big center scored 32 points to help Power Memorial win its third straight city title. His total of 2,067 points set an all-time city record. So did his 2,002 rebounds.

Lew was now looking forward to playing college basketball. But where would he go? Lew toured campuses and talked to coaches. It wasn't an easy decision for a 17-year-old to make.

The Best Team on Campus

In the spring of 1965, Lew held a press conference. He announced that he would attend college at the University of California at Los Angeles. Lew had not made a snap choice. He wanted to join a winning team—and UCLA had just won two straight national titles. Lew also liked the sunny, open campus. He said he'd seen more pretty girls there in a day than he'd see all summer in Central Park. UCLA also had a fine new basketball arena and an outstanding coach.

Coach John Wooden looked like a small-town schoolteacher. He wore glasses and parted his gray hair in the middle. Unlike some coaches, Wooden was calm and direct. He truly cared about his players. Basketball was important, he said, but so were good grades. That was what Lew wanted to hear.

Life in a college dorm was a hard adjustment for Lew. He was a private person and he missed having his own room. Down the hall, the washroom always seemed crowded with other athletes.

When he crossed the campus, students stared. That was a change from New York, where no one seemed to notice him. Lew said he felt like a sideshow freak. Going to school on a coed campus was also a new experience. Lew liked girls but felt shy when he was with them.

Lew's spirits lifted when basketball practice began. The freshman team could count on five high school All-Americans. One of them was Lew's roommate, Lucius Allen. Coach Gary Cunningham drilled the team in Coach Wooden's techniques. Practices went like clockwork, with no wasted time. Lew took part in all of the drills. He practiced lay-ups, fast breaks, hook shots and ball handling. Then he went one-on-one with assistant coach Jay Carty, a former Oregon State star. Carty gave Lew the same rough treatment he would receive from other teams. Lew took the jolts and bumps and came back for more. The pace was tiring. After practice each day he trudged back to his room to rest.

The **varsity** practiced at the other end of the gym. Wooden's veteran team was favored to win a third straight national championship. Could the freshmen keep up with these fine players and their pressure defense? UCLA basketball fans packed Pauley Pavilion to find out. When Lew and Lucius ran onto the floor people stared in amazement. At 6 feet 2 inches, Lucius Allen was not a small man. But Lew was a foot taller than the slick playmaking guard.

TRIVIA 3 | Even though he was 7 feet 2 inches, Kareem does not rank as the tallest player in basketball history. How does he compare with the tallest players ever seen on a basketball court?

USC's Ron Tayler watches in amazement as Lew Alcindor dunks the ball for the Bruins in this 1966 freshman game.

The game was never close. The varsity tried to put on its **full-court press**, but the frosh broke it easily. Lew took the inbound passes and handed off to Allen or Lynn Shackleford. Then he ran down court to take his place near the basket. If the varsity **double-teamed** him, Allen or Shackleford hit from the outside. When he was guarded one-on-one, Lew whirled to the basket for score after score. On defense, the frosh pressured the varsity into making a bushel of **turnovers**.

The final score was Frosh 75, Varsity 60. Lew had thrown in a game-high 31 points. After the fast start the freshmen went on to win all 21 of their games. Lew averaged 33.1 points a game to go with his 21.5 rebounds. The varsity was a fine team—but it wasn't the best team on campus.

THE UCLA GLORY DAYS

Lew Alcindor played his first varsity game in December 1967. When he took the floor, sportswriters were already calling him the nation's best player. The USC Trojans tried to play the young UCLA team man to man—always a big mistake. Lew scored a school record 56 points as the Bruins coasted to an easy 105-90 victory.

Injuries to his seniors forced Coach Wooden to start junior Cliff Warren and four sophs. The super sophs were Alcindor, Allen, Shackleford, and Kenny Heitz. Under Wooden's steady hand the team swept through its schedule without losing a game. Although some teams tried to freeze the ball, the tactic only kept the score down. Oregon held the Bruins to 40 points—but scored only 35 themselves.

Lew began his varsity career in this 1967 game against the USC Trojans. Pictured across from Lew is teammate Sidney Wicks (35).

UCLA won 30 games and a national title. The team's smallest margin of victory was five points. In the NCAA finals the Bruins blew a good Dayton team apart, 79-64. Lew lived up to his press clippings with a 29.7-points-a-game average. And he swept the boards clean with 15.5 rebounds a game.

TRIVIA 4

Kareem set an all-time college basketball record for field goal percentage during his sophomore year at UCLA. What percentage of his shots did he make that year?

Some sportswriters predicted that UCLA would never lose with Lew at center. The College Basketball Rules Committee tried to change the odds by banning the dunk shot. Lew did not like the rule change, but he adjusted to it. Instead of dunking, he banked in easy lay-ups when he went to the basket.

Seventeen wins later, UCLA met Houston in the Astrodome. Lew was not at his best after his eye injury, and Houston ended the win streak. But Coach Wooden had taught his team to keep its head up after a defeat. The Bruins roared back to win the rest of their games. After knocking off Houston in the semifinals, UCLA trounced North Carolina in the finals, 78-55. Lew's 34 points led the way.

Lew had been reading widely in Afro-American history. The books of Malcolm X held a special appeal for him. Malcolm was an American black who adopted the faith of Islam. Although raised a Catholic, Lew now converted to the Sunnite Muslim branch of Islam. At the same time he adopted the Islamic name Kareem Abdul-Jabbar. He did not make the change official, however, until three years later.

That summer, Lew turned down a chance to play for the U.S. Olympic basketball team. He chose to spend the summer working with Operation Sports Rescue. His job was teaching basketball to underprivileged kids. After each workout he talked to the young-sters about staying in school. Lew knew that only a handful of kids would earn their living by playing sports. Education was the best route out of the ghetto.

UCLA's Lew Alcindor shows underprivileged New York City kids how to hold a basketball for a dunk shot.

As a senior, Lew led the Bruins to their third straight NCAA title. The team lost only once that year. Crosstown rival USC used a slowdown game to pull off a 46-44 upset. In the NCAA tournament, Drake gave UCLA a scare before losing in the final seconds. That set up Lew's final college game against Purdue. The crowd was hoping to see an upset. As Lew said, "Nobody roots for Goliath." The big center's 37 points and an inspired defense produced a 92-72 victory.

As he waited for spring and graduation, Lew's thoughts turned to pro basketball. For the last three years he had lived in a tiny apartment. Spending money had been hard to come by. Now the pros were lining up to offer him big money to play the game he loved.

BREAKING IN WITH THE PROS

Pro teams cannot sign a player until they have **drafted** him. The team with the worst record from the past year gets first choice. In 1969 the **National Basketball Association's** Milwaukee Bucks won a coin flip that gave them the first pick. In the rival American Basketball Association the New York Nets picked first. Many fans thought Lew, who was homesick for New York, would sign with the Nets.

Lew did favor the Nets, but business was business. He said he would listen to only one offer from each team. The Bucks offered $1.4 million for five years. The Nets came in with only $1 million. Too late, the other ABA owners chipped in to raise the offer to $3.25 million. Lew would have liked the extra cash, but he had

Milwaukee Bucks' trainer, Arnie Garber, needed a chair to measure Lew for his team physical exam.

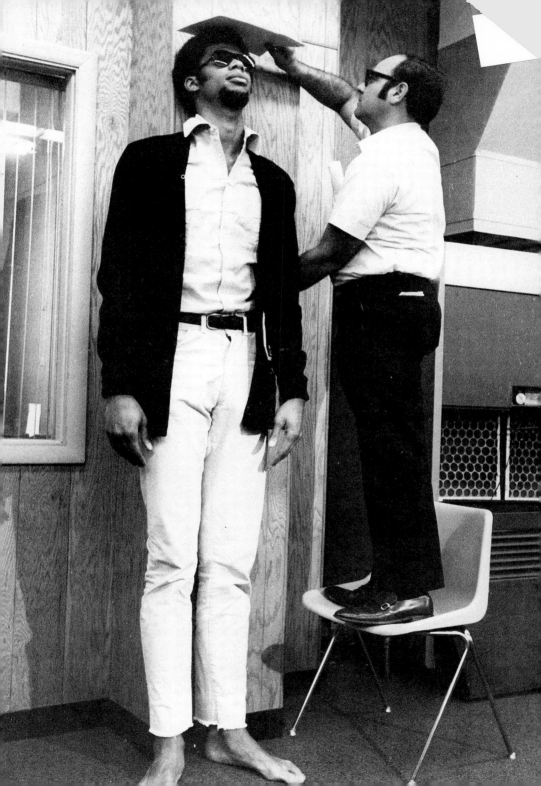

Milwaukee fans hoped that rookie Lew Alcindor would turn their team into a winner. Lew is shown here blocking the way for San Francisco Warrior, Nate Thurmond.

UCLA won three straight national championships in 1967, 1968 and 1969. Who was the MVP of the NCAA tournament in each of those years?

given his word. He turned down the ABA and signed with Milwaukee.

Lew looked forward to using the dunk shot again. Better yet, a team that didn't shoot within 24 seconds had to give up the ball. There was no stalling in this league. But could Lew hold his own against the league's big men? Some experts thought Wilt Chamberlain and Willis Reed would break him in two. Others said that the **rookie** was already the best big man in the game. Lew cautioned his fans to wait and see. "I'm going to have a lot to learn," he said.

The Bucks opened their season on October 18 against the Detroit Pistons. Lew's play excited the crowd. He scored 29 points as the Bucks won, 119-110. His defense was as important as his scoring. The scorebook showed 12 rebounds, three blocked shots, and three steals. At times Lew dribbled and passed the ball with the grace and skill of a **point guard**.

The area under the basket is a tough place to make a living. Lew was elbowed, held and stepped on. He had to fight back or be pushed off the floor. When the Philadelphia 76ers' Darrall Imhoff shoved him, Lew knocked Imhoff down. That same week he tangled with Willis Reed and Mike Riordan of the New York Knicks. Opposing players began to give him more room. Then came the big matchup with Wilt Chamberlain of the Los Angeles Lakers. The Bucks lost the game, but Lew held his own. He scored 23 points to Wilt's 25 and nabbed 20 rebounds to Wilt's 25.

Lew seemed to improve with each game. Over the 82-game season he led the Bucks to a second-place finish and a spot in the play-offs. After beating the 76ers, the Bucks came face to face with the Knicks. Lew scored 30 or more points in each game, but the Knicks won the series. The Knick coach had told his players that Lew would surely score 30 or more points. To win, the Knicks had to "stop everyone else."

After that loss the Bucks knew they needed more firepower. Before the 1970-1971 season the team traded for the great Oscar Robertson. The Big O was a high-scoring guard who could get the ball to Lew under the basket. The Bucks also obtained Lew's UCLA teammate and best friend, Lucius Allen. This was the year that Lew began to use his Islamic name. As Kareem Abdul-Jabbar he led the Bucks to 66 victories. His 31.7 points a game topped the NBA and won him **Most Valuable Player** honors.

Milwaukee opened the play-offs by sweeping past San Francisco and Los Angeles. The win over the Lakers put the Bucks in the finals against the Baltimore Bullets. The Bucks had never won a championship. They changed that by beating the Bullets in four straight games. Kareem had a fine series. No one argued when he was named the play-offs' MVP.

AN UNHAPPY MVP

Kareem's parents were hurt by his name change. Now there would be no one to carry on the family name. Kareem tried to explain that his belief in Islam had made him a new person. He told reporters that Abdul-Jabbar means "the powerful servant of Allah." Kareem took another big step that same spring. He married Habiba, the former Janice Brown. She gave him three children in the years that followed.

24

Kareem Abdul-Jabbar is pictured here with his bride, Habiba, following their 1971 wedding.

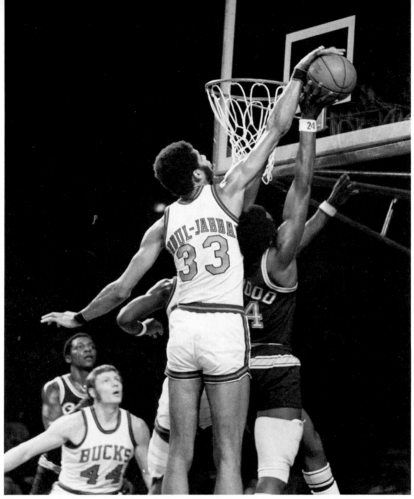

Kareem's height advantage helped him to block his opponents' shots with ease.

On the court, fans were cheering Kareem's deadly sky hook. To release the shot, Kareem launched himself into the air and extended his long right arm. Then he hooked the ball back over his head. As Kareem explained, "You can't defend against it. Nobody can get a hand on it." Most centers crash the lane and take a beating on their way to the basket. Kareem calmly stepped away from the crush and flipped in his sky hooks.

In 1971-1972 Kareem once more led the league in scoring, with 34.8 points a game. He was third in rebounding, with 16.6 rebounds a game. For the second straight year he was voted the NBA's Most Valuable Player. But Number 33 could not do it all by himself. The Bucks lost to the Los Angeles Lakers in the semifinals.

Losing the championship was not the only thing that upset Kareem. He disliked the cold weather in Milwaukee. Even more, he felt out of place. People pointed at him and gawked when he went shopping. More and more, he hid his feelings. On the team bus Kareem pulled his coat over his head and listened to jazz tapes. Religion was another comfort. Five times each day he faced toward **Mecca** and said his prayers.

Life in Wisconsin did not improve in 1972-1973. A jinx seemed to haunt the team. Lucius Allen was arrested on a drug charge. Oscar Robertson was slowed down by aches and pains. Coach Larry Costello claimed he had a full roster for only one game that season. Despite their problems, the Bucks rallied behind Kareem to win 60 games. But in the NBA it's the play-offs that count. The Golden State Warriors ended the Bucks' season in the first round.

Kareem and the Bucks came back strong in 1973-1974. Kareem won his third MVP award and the unofficial title of best center in basketball. The Bucks rolled through the play-offs and

TRIVIA 6

UCLA produced two of the greatest centers who ever played college and pro basketball, Kareem Abdul-Jabbar and Bill Walton. If fame can be measured by counting the number of times a player has appeared on the cover of *Sports Illustrated* who comes out ahead?

met the Boston Celtics in the finals. In the sixth game Kareem hit a sky hook in double overtime to tie the series. The Celtics' game plan for the seventh game was to keep the ball away from Kareem. The plan worked well enough to give them the game and the title.

The 1974-1975 season was a disaster. Kareem sat out six weeks after he broke two bones in his hand. Angry at being gouged in the eye, he punched the backboard support. It was a stupid thing to do, he admitted. After the eye injury, he wore wraparound goggles to protect his eyes. The goggles gave him a man-from-space look.

With their star sidelined, the Bucks fell out of the play-off picture. Kareem asked to be traded after the season ended. He was tired of trying to carry the team on his back. Although the Bucks didn't want to lose him, they knew he meant what he said. Several teams wanted Kareem, but the best offer came from Los Angeles.

TRIVIA 7

Kareem scored 56 points in his first game with the UCLA varsity in 1966. How many times did he surpass that first game in terms of points scored? What was his high-point game as a college player?

Lakers players and fans counted on Kareem to give their team a much needed boost. Here, Kareem drives past the Bucks' Alton Lister with Lakers' Byron Scott nearby.

STARTING OVER IN LOS ANGELES

The Lakers were a team in trouble when Kareem joined them. Gail Goodrich and Lucius Allen (obtained from the Bucks) were quick, but small. The forwards could not be counted on for much muscle under the boards. Players came and went as the coaches shuffled through 17 starting lineups. The Lakers and their fans welcomed Kareem. Could he turn the team into a winner?

Kareem put on the purple Laker uniform and went to work. Despite the turmoil on the team he rang up some splendid stats. Goggles and all, he led the NBA in rebounding and finished second in scoring. For the fourth time in six years, the league voted him its MVP. Despite Kareem's fine play, the Lakers lost more games than they won that year. The owners knew they had to rebuild.

The ABA closed down after the 1975-1976 season. The Lakers saw their chance. After cutting six veterans, the team signed four ABA players and brought in two rookies. The team also hired a new coach, former Laker star Jerry West. West told Kareem that his new teammates would make playing fun again.

Kareem holds his finger up to reporters to show that his team will soon be number one.

For outside shooting, the Lakers could count on Earl Tatum, Cazzie Russell, and Lucius. Forward Kermit Washington stepped up to help with the rebounding. Freed of some of his work load, Kareem polished a turnaround jump shot. Inspired by Kareem's goggles, writers were soon calling it the moonball.

Basketball experts did not expect much from the 1976-1977 Lakers. The team changed a lot of minds when it won 33 of its first 50 games. That fast start included a 20-game win streak at home. The good feelings vanished during the play-offs. After the Lakers lost to Seattle in four straight, fans laid the blame on Kareem. Sportscasters charged that he was getting old and lazy.

Kareem shrugged off the bad press. He knew the Lakers would soon be back on top. Besides, he was enjoying California. At age 30 he had a new home and time to enjoy the warm weather. His unhappy marriage to Habiba had broken up. Living near Hollywood gave him a chance to start a new career as an actor. Television viewers tuned in to see him on "Mannix" and "Emergency!"

Early in the 1977-1978 season the Lakers gave Kareem a lifetime contract. The team's faith in its star didn't cure his hot temper. After Milwaukee's Kent Benson elbowed him in the stomach, Kareem punched the rookie in the head. The blow knocked Benson down—and broke Kareem's hand again. He missed 19 games while the hand was in a cast. For a while he was depressed enough to think about quitting.

TRIVIA 8

Wilt Chamberlain holds the NBA single-season record for rebounds with a total of 2,149. Who holds second place?

Kareem reaches for the basket as his opponents try unsuccessfully to block him.

It was at that low point that Cheryl Pistono came into Kareem's life. When Cheryl gave him advice, he listened. She helped him control his temper and make himself more open to people. "Your life is not a jail sentence," she told him. In time Cheryl became more than a friend and counselor. Kareem fell in love with her, and she gave birth to his fourth child, Amir.

The Lakers made the play-offs in 1978 and again in 1979. Each time the team fell short. Kareem was still looking for his second championship ring. The Lakers knew they needed a star point guard to put them over the top.

KAREEM TEAMS WITH MAGIC

The Lakers found the key to "winnin' time" by drafting Earvin (Magic) Johnson in 1979. The 6-foot-9-inch guard was a magician with a basketball. Better yet, Magic's zest for playing basketball improved everyone's game. Guard Norm Nixon and forwards Jamaal Wilkes and Spencer Haywood completed the starting lineup. Michael Cooper was a perfect **sixth man** coming off the bench.

For Kareem, basketball was fun again. In the season opener he sank a sky hook at the buzzer to beat San Diego. As he turned to trot off the floor, Magic leaped into his arms and gave him a bear hug. "Hey, we got 81 more [games]," Kareem scolded. Even so, he had to admit that making the last shot had been exciting.

Led by Kareem and Magic, the Lakers won the western division. Then they rolled through the play-offs, defeating Phoenix and Seattle. In the finals they were matched against

Julius (Dr. J) Erving's Philadelphia 76ers. The teams split the first four games. In the third quarter of the fifth game, Kareem twisted his ankle. He told the trainer to tape the ankle and then limped back to the court. Despite the pain, Kareem scored 14 fourth-quarter points to help the Lakers win by 5.

Kareem was forced to sit out the sixth game. His teammates did not let him down. With Magic playing center and scoring 42 points, the Lakers blitzed the 76ers, 123-107. A few days later, Kareem was named the regular-season MVP. It was his sixth MVP trophy, a league record.

Magic went down with a knee injury early in the 1981-1982 season. The team never recovered, even after the big guard returned. All the pieces fell into place the next year. Once again the Lakers destroyed the 76ers and won their second title in three years. This time Kareem was there to enjoy the victory party.

The Lakers were aiming at back-to-back titles, but 1982-1983 was not their year. In January Kareem's home burned while he was on the road. Cheryl and Amir escaped unhurt, but Kareem lost his jazz albums, his priceless **Korans**, and a lifetime of memories. To his surprise, people all over the country wrote to express their sympathy. A radio station sent a truck loaded with 1,500 jazz records. Kareem, who so often kept the world at arm's length, was touched. People he had never met really cared about him.

An injury-riddled Laker team won a spot in the play-offs. Rookie forward James Worthy was emerging as a bright new star. But the quest for a repeat victory ran into a detour in the finals. The 76ers gained their revenge by taking the title away from the Lakers in four straight.

Kareem proudly shows off his sixth Most Valuable Player trophy.

On April 5, 1984, Kareem sank a sky hook against the Utah Jazz. The basket ran his point total to 31,421 and broke Chamberlain's record. Despite these heroics, Kareem and his Lakers lost to Boston in the 1984 finals. But they came back to even the score by beating the Celtics in 1985. *Sports Illustrated* named Kareem as its Man of the Year.

After winning again in 1987, the Lakers gave Kareem a new contract worth $5 million. Laker fans wondered if the big man would retire when the contract ran out in 1989.

THE FINAL YEAR

Kareem confirmed that he would retire after the 1988-1989 season. Ten years earlier, he would have left quietly. Now a more open and relaxed Kareem agreed to the idea of a farewell tour. Every team in the NBA began planning a night in his honor. The fans wanted to say good-bye to one of the giants of the game.

The tour began in New York. Just being in the Big Apple brought back special memories. This was the city where 8-year-old Lew Alcindor had first played basketball. It was here that he had starred for Power Memorial.

TRIVIA 9 Kareem set his last NBA record in his final season, even though he averaged only 10.1 points a game. What record did he set in 1988-1989.

Kareem demonstrates his dunk shot while scoring two points for the Lakers.

During the halftime ceremony, the announcer spoke for all the cheering fans. "Tonight's guest of honor, in his...twentieth and final NBA season," the voice boomed out. "Six-time NBA Most Valuable Player, six-time member of NBA championship teams, the greatest scorer in the history of the game..." Then, after a pause, "Let's say thanks...with one last Madison Square Garden salute, to the master of the sky hook, future Hall of Famer, Kareem Abdul-Jabbar!"

At 42, Kareem had beaten long odds just to be playing at all. The average NBA career ends after four years. Even if a player doesn't blow out a knee, the body takes a fierce pounding. Top-flight basketball is a game of sudden stops and starts and high-speed turns. Every play puts stress on knees, ankles and feet. After jumping, a player hits the floor with a force equal to 12 times his body weight. Stress fractures of the foot are a growing problem.

Kareem had his own ideas on how to stay healthy. Unlike most players, he refused to let trainers tape his ankles. Taping, he said, passes the stress on to the knees. Before every practice and game, he went through a set of stretching routines. In the off-season he stayed in shape by jumping rope and swimming. He also worked with weights and kept to a strict diet. Another of Kareem's secrets was his ability to "focus his energy and harness his power." He used techniques taught by Bruce Lee, a star of martial arts films.

TRIVIA 10

Kareem holds a number of important NBA regular-season records. How many can you name?

Kareem Abdul-Jabbar waves goodbye to his fans after 20 years in the NBA.

The Lakers did not let Kareem's good-bye tour take their minds off their goal. After winning in 1987 and 1988, they wanted a third straight NBA title. Coach Pat Riley called it their "three-peat." For a time it looked as though the team would give Kareem one last championship ring. The Lakers marched into the finals by winning 11 straight games. That feat set up a rematch of the 1988 series with the "bad boys" of the Detroit Pistons.

The Laker's luck ran out one series too soon. Before the first game, Byron Scott went down with a **hamstring** injury. Without Scott's sharpshooting, the Lakers lost, 109-97. Then Magic went down in the second game. James Worthy missed a last-second foul shot, and Detroit won again. Kareem did his best to bring his team back in game three. He scored 24 points, but it wasn't enough to hold off the Pistons. Kareem's career ended on a low note as Detroit ran off with the fourth game and the title.

The crowd chanted "Kareem! Kareem! Kareem!" as Number 33 walked off the court. The fans knew they were watching the end of a legendary career.

KAREEM ABDUL-JABBAR, BASKETBALL IMMORTAL

Sunday, April 23, 1989, was a special day at the Forum in Inglewood, California. A sellout crowd packed the arena even though the Lakers had already wrapped up a conference title. The fans were there to honor a basketball immortal.

The voice of Laker broadcaster Chick Hearn silenced the crowd. When Hearn announced Kareem's name the arena rocked with cheers. Kareem was led to a seat in a giant rocking chair. His youngest son, Amir, sang the national anthem.

Hearn read a telegram from President George Bush. Then Kareem's teammates stepped forward to sing a musical tribute. When the silliness was over, Magic handed Kareem a set of keys. "Since you've been carrying us on your back for all these years," Magic said, "we decided to get something that would carry you." The "something" was a $175,000 white Rolls-Royce. An Inglewood official announced that the street beside the Forum would be renamed Kareem Court. Laker owner Jerry Buss promised to build a tennis court on Kareem's land in Hawaii.

At last it was Kareem's turn at the mike. He thanked his parents for setting high standards for him to live by. He singled out a grade school teacher and his early coaches for special praise. Then he thanked his teammates and the fans for their support. In closing he said, "I'm losing my voice. I want to say I love you all."

The Laker girls showed up in T-shirts printed with Kareem's famous 33. The other Lakers wore copies of Kareem's goggles. That day, the Lakers beat Seattle by four, 121-117. Kareem scored his final regular season points on a pass from Magic. Those last points brought his total to 38,387.

After the game, Kareem was called on to do some interviews. While he answered questions, his teammates shredded his street clothes with scissors. The guest of honor had to drive home in his sweat suit.

Kareem enjoys his new life away from basketball. He has time to rest, read and pursue new projects. When rookie centers enter the NBA he knows they will be measured against his 20 years of great play. He says he remembers his playing years with pride. "I won't be able to taste those moments again," he says, "but they will not be forgotten."

GLOSSARY

boarding school—A school that houses and feeds its students in addition to giving them classroom instruction.

double-team—The tactic of assigning two defensive players to guard the opposing team's top scorer.

draft—A system by which pro teams take turns selecting the top college stars from each year's crop of eligible players. The team with the worst record drafts first.

dunk shot—A shot in which a player jumps high enough to slam the ball through the hoop with a downward motion.

full-court press—A tactic in which the defensive players pressure the offense from the moment the ball is put into play.

hamstring—Either of the two large tendons found at the back of the upper leg. A hamstring injury can put a basketball player out of action for several weeks.

Koran—The holy book of the Muslim faith. Muslims believe the Koran contains the words of Allah as revealed to Mohammed.

Mecca—A holy city in Saudi Arabia. Devout Muslims face toward Mecca when they pray.

Most Valuable Player (MVP)—An award given each year to the league's best player.

National Basketball Association (NBA)—The "major leagues" of pro basketball. The winner of each year's NBA play-offs is considered the best team in basketball.

National Collegiate Athletic Association (NCAA)—The organization that supervises college athletics. The NCAA sponsors the yearly tournament that determines the national college basketball champions.

point guard—The player who brings the ball down court and runs the offense. A point guard's job is similar to that of a quarterback in football.

rebound—To take possession of the ball after it bounces off the rim or backboard following a missed shot.

rookies—Athletes who are playing for the first time at the major-league level.

sixth man—A player whose skills are almost as good as those of the starters. Coaches send the sixth man into a game to guard an opposing player who is "hot," or to generate some instant offense.

turnovers—Mistakes by the offensive team that allow the defensive team to take control of the ball.

varsity—The highest level team in a sports program. The best players are assigned to the varsity.

MORE GOOD READING ABOUT KAREEM

Abdul-Jabbar, Kareem and Peter Knobler. *Giant Steps*. New York: Bantam Books, 1983.

Abdul-Jabbar, Kareem with Mignon McCarthy. *Kareem*. New York: Random House, 1990.

Carpenter, Jerry and Steve DiMeglio. *Kareem Abdul-Jabbar*. Minneapolis: ABDO and Daughters, 1988.

Haskins, James. *From Lew Alcindor to Kareem Abdul-Jabbar*. New York: Lothrop, Lee and Stephard Books, 1978.

Ostler, Scott and Steve Springer. *Winnin' Times; the Magical Journey of the Los Angeles Lakers*. New York: Macmillan Publishing Co., 1986.

Pepe, Phil. *Stand Tall: the Lew Alcindor Story*. New York: Grosset & Dunlap, 1970.

Wooden, John. *They Call Me Coach*. Waco, TX: Word Books, 1972.

KAREEM ABDUL-JABBAR TRIVIA QUIZ

1: Kareem was given the lowly task of carrying the ball bag to and from practice. In later years, Kareem agreed that Donohue did the right thing. "I wasn't treated any differently than anybody else on the team," he said.

2: The Boys High player bit Kareem on the arm. When Kareem showed the teeth marks to the referee, the biter was thrown out of the game.

3: The tallest player to make the NBA is 7-foot-6 3/4-inch Manute Bol. The tallest player in the history of the game was Suleiman Ali Nashmush. Suleiman was said to be 8 feet tall when he played for Libya in 1962.

4: Kareem was credited with a field goal percentage of .667 in 1966-1967. That means he made two out of every three shots he tried from the field.

5: Kareem was named MVP of all three tournaments. Records are made to be broken, but this one will very likely endure.

6: Kareem wins the *Sports Illustrated* competition hands down. He has appeared on the magazine's cover 27 times. Walton has appeared only 14 times.

7: Kareem exceeded his first-game total of 56 points only once during his college career. He scored a school-record 61 points against Washington State in 1967.

8: Wilt had no peers as a rebounder. He also holds the second, third, fourth, fifth, sixth and seventh places! Bill Russell is the eighth-place rebounder. Kareem's best year as a rebounder was 1975-1976, when he pulled down 1,383 rebounds.

9: Kareem was 42 years old when he played in 74 games for the Lakers that year. No one else that old has ever played regularly for an NBA team.

10: Kareem holds the following NBA regular-season records:
Most points scored—38,387
Most games played—1,560
Most times selected MVP—6
Most field goals made—15,837
Most blocked shots—3,189
Most personal fouls—4,657
Most seasons played—20

index

Abdul-Jabbar, Amir 33, 34, 41
Alabama 12
Alcindor, Cora 7
Alcindor, Al 7
All-Americans 14
Allen, Lucius 14, 16, 24, 27, 29, 31
American Basketball Association (ABA) 20, 23

Baltimore Bullets 24
Benson, Kent 31
Boston Celtics 28, 37
Bush, President George 41
Buss, Jerry 41

Carty, Jay 14
Central Park 13
Chamberlain, Wilt 23, 37
College Basketball Rules Committee 18
Cooper, Michael 33
Costello, Larry 27
Cunningham, Gary 14

Detroit Pistons 23, 40
Donohue, Jack 11
Dyckman Housing Project 7

Erving, Julius (Dr. J) 34
"Emergency" 31

Fort Tryon Park 7

Golden State Warriors 27
Goodrich, Gail 29

Habiba (Janice Brown) 24, 31
Hayes, Elvin (Big E) 5, 6
Haywood, Spencer 33
Hearn, Chick 41
Heitz, Kenny 16
Holy Providence 8
Hopkins, Farrell 8
Houston Cougars 5, 6, 18
Hudson River 11

Imhoff, Darrall 23
Inglewood, California 41
Islam 18, 24

Johnson, Earvin (Magic) 33, 34, 40, 41

Kareem Court 41

Lee, Bruce 38
Los Angeles Lakers 23, 24, 27, 28, 29, 30, 31,
   33, 34, 37, 40, 41

Madison Square Garden 11, 38
Malcolm X 18
"Mannix" 31
Mecca 27
Milwaukee Bucks 20, 23, 24, 27, 28
Milwaukee, Wisconsin 27
Most Valuable Player 24, 27, 30, 34

National Basketball Association (NBA) 20, 24, 27, 30,
   37, 38, 40, 42
NCAA 6, 17, 20
New York, New York 7, 8
New York 11, 37
New York Knicks 23, 24
New York Nets 20
Nixon, Norm 33
North Carolina 6, 12, 18

Operation Sports Rescue 18

Pauley Pavilion 14
Philadelphia 76ers 23, 34
Philadelphia, Pennsylvania 7
Pistono, Cheryl 33, 34
Power Memorial Academy 8, 10, 11, 37
Power Memorial Academy Panthers 11, 13

Reed, Willis 23
Riley, Pat 40
Riordan, Mike 23
Robertson, Oscar 24, 27
Roy's Coffee Shop 8
Russell, Cazzie 31

St. Jude 7, 8
Scott, Byron 40
Shackleford, Lynn 16
Sports Illustrated 37
Sunnite Muslim 18

Tatum, Earl 31

UCLA Bruins 5, 6, 16, 17, 18, 20
U.S. Olympic Basketball Team 18
University of California at Los Angeles (UCLA) 13, 14
USC Trojans 16, 20

Warren, Cliff 16
Washington, Kermit 31
West, Jerry 30
Wilkes, Jamaal 33
Wooden, John 13, 18
Worthy, James 34, 40

JAN   1997